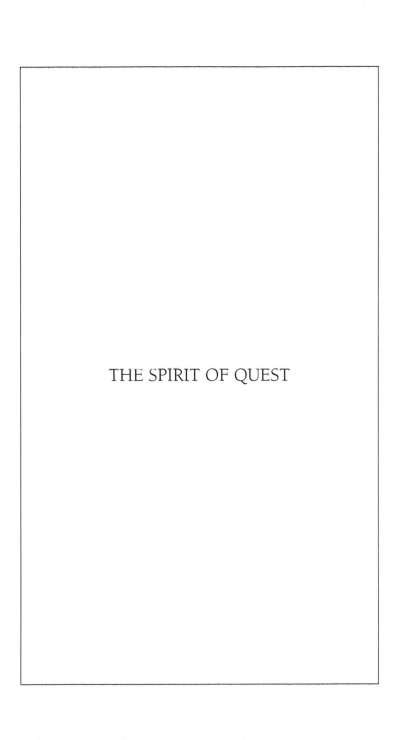

THE SPIRIT OF QUEST

The Spirit of Quest

Essays and Poems

D.M. DOOLING

Illustrations by Angela Laignel

PARABOLA BOOKS • NEW YORK • 1994

THE SPIRIT OF QUEST: ESSAYS AND POEMS
By D.M. Dooling

A PARABOLA Book, February 1994

The essays in this volume were originally published in PARABOLA,
The Magazine of Myth and Tradition, between 1976 and 1990.

"The Crystal Skull" was originally published in PARABOLA,
The Magazine of Myth and Tradition, II:1, 1977.

"Sagebrush" and "August" were originally published in *The New Republic,* 1928.

PARABOLA BOOKS is a publishing division of The Society for the Study of
Myth and Tradition, a not-for-profit organization devoted to the
dissemination and exploration of materials related to myth, symbol,
ritual, and art of the great religious traditions. The Society also publishes
PARABOLA, *The Magazine of Myth and Tradition.*

ISBN   0–930407–30-X

PARABOLA BOOKS
656 Broadway • New York, NY 10012

Design by Martin Moskof
Manufactured in the United States of America

FOREWORD

I n the winter of 1976 PARABOLA, a quarterly devoted to
Myth and the Quest for Meaning, made its first
appearance. It was the brainchild of Dorothea Matthews
Dooling.

"PARABOLA has a conviction," she wrote in an intro-
duction to the inaugural issue, "that human existence is
significant, that life essentially makes sense in spite of our
confusions, that man is not here on earth by accident but
for a purpose, and that whatever that purpose may be it
demands from him the discovery of his own meaning, his
own totality and identity. A human being is born to set out
on this quest, his quest, like a knight of Arthur's court."
That essay by the magazine's founder and editor-publisher
was the first of a series. Each issue of PARABOLA has been
devoted to the great thematic questions—Creation, The
Child, Initiation, Earth and Spirit, Ceremonies, Pilgrimage, Wholeness, Old Age, Exile, Death. To address these
questions Dooling enlisted a sequence of authors and thinkers
including Isaac Bashevis Singer, Joseph Campbell, Ursu-
la K. Le Guin, Frederick Franck, Joseph Epes Brown, Helen
M. Luke, Gary Snyder, Elaine Pagels, Peter Brook, P.L. Travers, Mircea Eliade, Elaine Jahner, H.H. the Dalai Lama,
Peter Matthiessen, Sister Maria José Hobday, Richard
Neibuhr, Elie Wiesel, and Laurens van der Post. Along-
side such contributors were relevant passages gleaned from
sacred texts throughout history.

However challenging the subject or formidable the company, Dooling managed in each introductory "Focus" to leave the reader both edified and reassured. She was a true believer in the sense of being precisely on pitch and her writing was informed by an unshakable and unsentimental optimism. These brief essays add up to a working credo for a twentieth-century pilgrim whose search continued until her death in 1991.

What manner of woman was this who achieved such a precise wisdom and guided a publication of such distinction and weight?

When I first met her in the early PARABOLA years, Dorothea Dooling was a handsome white-haired woman with presence, a Michelangelo sibyl, a grand dame with curiosity and compassion, a woman who knew a lot but was not oppressive in her wisdom, a considerate leader who would always pursue with the same enthusiasm the quest she began as a young woman.

She was born to privilege: the youngest child of Elsie Procter Matthews (of Procter and Gamble), and Paul Matthews, an episcopal clergyman soon to be consecrated Bishop of New Jersey. After a private school education she enrolled in Somerville College, Oxford, where in her second year, in her own words, she "became more and more ill at ease . . . The female undergraduates are very much looked down on: they are most unattractively intellectual, and their presence at the University is resented by the men. To make them feel even more inferior they have to wear hideous caps. I began to feel curiously oppressed and overwhelmed by the male element and my own inferior position among them."

Her answer was to retreat to the Northwest mountains of the U.S., marry, and raise a family. After twenty-two years as a ranch wife in Montana, where she schooled her six children at home, she returned east as a single mother. There, when time permitted, she pursued a course of independent study, research, and writing. At age sixty-five she began the magazine which over the next decade and a half grew to a circulation of more than forty thousand.

Although as a Bishop's daughter she had been grounded in the Christian faith, Dorothea Dooling adhered to no single creed. Over the years she had made it her business to familiarize herself with all traditions. Among myths she was particularly moved by those of the natives of the Plains, the Southwest, and Central America; but to her all myths were instructive, "never defining, always throwing light." Among contemporary thinkers she was drawn to the teaching of the Russian savant Gurdjieff whom she had met in 1948. But she was indifferent to no one whom she judged enlightened. It was this catholicity of interest, this receptivity to all spiritual voices which informed her own life and the magazine she founded.

The volume ends appropriately with a sheaf of Dooling poems, giving another side of her remarkable character.

Reading these essays and poems, one gets some small notion of the reach and depth of a great spirit.

Marvin Barrett
Water Mill, New York
August, 1993

CONTENTS

THE SPIRIT OF QUEST

CREATION

THE HERO

Who is the hero, that more-than-life-sized figure of myth and history and fairy tale; the conqueror of evil, the liberator, the rescuer of the oppressed? How terrible to think of not being the hero of one's own life; this is the role for which each of us is cast, no matter how unsuccessfully we play it. And if the part seems too big, if we picture the hero as being indeed "more than life-sized," it is because our daily life has dwindled, become less than real, and only pygmy proportions seem natural to us.

Every true teaching, every genuine tradition has sought to train its disciples to act this part, to become in fact followers of the great quest for one's self. Saint or sannyasin, monk or craft apprentice, Sioux sun-dance warrior, Muslim sheikh, or knight of the Round Table, all are striving for the conquest of the ego-dragon, the finding and liberating of the pure essence, the center of being. As Mircea Eliade has shown in Images and Symbols, the search for centrality expressed in myths and rituals across the globe is the search for the truly human position, the midpoint and link between heaven and hell, angel and animal; the specifically human function of the reconciliation of the opposites, by which life becomes whole and holy, eternal, no longer divided, and at last "makes sense." The search for salvation, or immortality, however we understand those terms, is first and foremost the search for that in oneself that is more than mortal.

Every person is a potential hero, even ourselves, and every society, even our own, is a potential training ground for those who recognize and accept their role. This recognition may be buried deeply in the subconscious, yet it expresses itself today in our torn and dying world as it has throughout time, if we can learn how to decode the messages of myths ancient and modern, of our own customs, our own actions and our own dreams. This world we live in, with its brutal protectorates and its law-breaking legislators, its crusades for freedom leading to worse slaveries, this world of murderous contradiction, destruction, competition—this world we live in needs our heroism as it has never before been needed in human memory. How to be heroes today? Who will help us to learn, or give us the magic gifts that win the treasure in the fairy tale?

So our search begins by looking for help; and here we find that not everything that offers help can be trusted; the enemy puts on many disguises, and even before courage we need a keen eye and a keen nose. Indeed, for the ancient Maya the capacity not to be fooled was the hero's first requisite. So a constant watchfulness is needed, a certain skepticism, and a refusal of stereotyped definitions. The followers of the traditions (though not their teachers) tend to stake claims on truth that are mutually exclusive, and to add their interpretations to scripture. But Christ and Buddha, Moses and Mohammed, were not giving personal opinions, nor speaking of different things. If truth is one, where is the center, the hub of the wheel, the place where all teachings meet at their source? Perhaps the only access point is at the source and center of oneself.

The study of myths and symbols will serve us only in throwing light on our unknown selves. It is not an academic study; the effort to decipher our own unconscious symbols, unravel the real meanings behind our actions, witness unblinkingly the parts we actually play, exacts from us an exercise both of courage and of discrimination that can perhaps be the beginning of our training for the starring role we were intended for.

COSMOLOGY

A series of irrelevant incidents had brought me, for the first time in my life, into a college astronomy lecture. It was long before the days of audio-visual teaching techniques, but the lecturer had invented his own. He leapt from one contraption to another with an attention-riveting agility. First it was a projector showing a series of slides which, he explained, had been taken by a fixed camera that recorded the position of each of the planets at the same hour every night for a year. The graph of each periodic movement made a different pattern: asymmetric, sometimes very beautiful, with darting lines and strange curves like exotic flowers. Then he sprang to the blackboard, and showed how the same planetary paths would look as seen from a central point, instead of from the oblique viewpoint of a spot on the surface of one of their own number.

"If you were standing on the sun with your camera," he said, "the patterns would all come out like this," and he drew on the blackboard a series of continuous horizontal lines, interrupted at more or less regular intervals by larger or smaller loops. He beamed at the class.

"Such a repetition would seem to show the operation of a law, wouldn't it?" he said. "Now what law would produce that unfailing result?"

He turned like a tiddlywink to another blackboard and another subject, the swinging motion of the pendulum. The pendulum demonstrates a vibration, he said—a back and forth movement of unequal speed, for it slows down at two points: one as it approaches its farthest limit, the other as it begins its downward swing. All movements, he added, produce vibrations, and all vibrations can be supposed to produce sound, though between the highest pitched, the smallest and most rapid ones, and the lowest, which are larger and slower, only a small range is audible to the human ear, while some animals are able to hear a little above or below the sounds perceptible to us.

Now he left the blackboard, and on one side of the room swiftly rigged up a double pendulum: a horizontal broomstick tied with cords to a hot water pipe in the ceiling, and another similar one suspended from the first. To the lower one he attached an open-ended glass cone filled with sand; put both pendulums in motion—one north and south, the other east and west—and drew a long strip of blue paper beneath them; the sand trickling from the swinging glass wrote on the paper the long circling line of the movement of the planets.

It was the end of the hour. The professor beamed again and disappeared without a word, leaving the unspoken questions hanging in the room behind him. The vibrations of the planets? What ear can hear so huge a sound? And what about us, Professor? Where are we in the music of the spheres?

The vision of a harmonious universe shows everything in its right place, with one exception. Human beings seem to be the only living things that have to question themselves, that don't know who they are nor what they are for. Plants and animals fulfill their function without discussion, unless we interfere with them. It is only we who don't know what to do with ourselves: we have forgotten our lines, and there is no prompter. We drift onstage like people struck with amnesia, not knowing our own name, nor how to find ourselves again.

Yet our memory is not totally gone; it is cut, there is a terrible break, but there are some memories of our past. There was a "time before the fall," before the forgetting; a moment when humans were closer to their "names," to the notes they were designed to sound. We have memory-glimpses, as if it were a dream-taste of our own childhood, of a golden age in which humans lived "in harmony" with their surroundings. But our present is cacophonous. We are as out of tune with nature as with each other and ourselves, and we begin to be afraid; we begin to see the disharmony as at least partly of our own making, and to recognize that these discordant vibrations could destroy the very planet we live on. Our whole world is a Jericho whose walls are tumbling down. Will our dissonance destroy us? Or is there another, truer note within our range, a resolving chord through which we could find our balance again in the rhythm and melody of creation? What vibration is proper to us? Perhaps we can remember, rather than invent, the answers; perhaps a deliberate searching in the past can help us understand our inexplicable present.

In the fairy story, the door of the subterranean cave can be opened only by the reverberation of a magic word. Before the seeker can enter the chamber where the treasure lies, he or she must recall this word; recall it, or perhaps be called back to it, but this cannot happen through the help of any other person, only through its echo within. No one can tell the seeker what it is, for it is at once the Unpronounceable Name, and the unique vibration of his or her own individual planet.

SACRED SPACE

Very little seems sacred nowadays, and space has come to mean an "outer space" too vast for habitation except for NASA's beeping satellites. So what relevance can "sacred space" have for us today? The sacred has been defined as the "wholly other." It does not deny our ordinary reality, but is its other aspect: it completes it and makes it whole or "holy." It is the force that joins us to another level. And a real force does seem to linger in some of the dedicated places of the past. The scalp prickles when we pass a certain ancient doorway; we shiver, spine-chilled, in such a spot as the ceremonial cavern at Bandelier; the voice drops to a whisper when we enter Chartres. There is a sense of recognition, sometimes of sudden fear, on crossing the unmarked boundary of what don Juan called a "place of power."

When we examine our own experience as well as the records left to us in earth and stone, we see that sacred space is not just any space; it must be defined by something, and contained by this definition. It is enclosed by boundaries which are not necessarily walls and a roof; its boundaries are the boundaries of power. There are still such places. But what is the power with which they affect us? Perhaps it is a magic whose secret has been forgotten, but a secret still decipherable in the symbolism through which we are permitted to approach it.

For a space to be impregnated by that Otherness, it

must be empty—a Void, a womb where life can be begotten, where something can take place. The power which enters it (the sun's rays at a certain moment of the solstice; the spring that bubbles up) is the power of creation and of becoming. And the form which defines this space, whether it be that of temple, dolmen, or holy mountain, the ritual lodge or the sacred mound or cavern, in one way or another always seems to symbolize the form of the human being. "Ye are the temple of God," said St. Paul to the Corinthians, and to us.

To accept this saying would be no light thing; it would mean a return to the outlook of the traditions, of religious man and his acceptance of a relationship which entails a heavy responsibility. Even to consider it as a possibility would make it necessary to take a very different view of the holy places, and of what took place there. The rites that were practiced in many, even most of them, we will never know, and certainly we would not dare to imitate what is still done, for instance, in the kiva of the Hopi Snake Clan. But that is not the point, if we look in a new way; for we see that the importance of the sacred places does not rest in either of the two ways we may have thought of them before. They are not simply relics of the past that can teach us of other races and other times; nor are they the hiding places of magical rites which, could we discover them, would automatically create miracles for us. Their value for us is much more real and more practical, for they speak (in riddles, to be sure) of us and our own functionings.

How can we find an interior "space," our own place of possible becoming? What is born, what is worshipped, what is sacrificed, in this temple? What force is generated, and what instantaneous event or lifelong process could be the destined result of this causal power? In this epoch of search for oneself, is some sort of clue to be found here? Perhaps we are, in fact, simply and miraculously, places where something could happen.

MAGIC

L eave nothing to what is called luck and you will be what is called lucky" is a homely saying that says something rather important about what we refer to as chance, or accident. It tells us, in fact, that there is no such thing, and that none of the excuses it authorizes for us are valid. Accidents are simply the results of unseen, or unforeseen, causes. They break the rules of our generalized expectations, but not the inexorable laws of cause and effect.

This is what seems—but only seems—puzzling about magic. Magic, when it is not just trickery, seems to play with laws, to make the magician's will the supreme agent. The word itself comes from a root meaning "to be able, to have power." The magician is the magus, the mighty one, the worker of miracles. What then is magic, what is a miracle? Where does the power come from? What laws is it above, what laws is it under? For in the hierarchy of nature we know of nothing below the divine Absolute that does not obey the higher cause. What are the laws of magic?

The French alchemist Jollivet-Castelot says: "Magic is rational, positive, for it proclaims the constancy of natural laws; but it teaches that the field of operation of these laws is infinite and that most of them are still unknown to men." The laws we see are the results of laws we cannot see.

Magicians range from Carlos Castaneda's possessors of knowledge to the dark powers of Xibalba, and the process of their art from psychological reassurance or disintegration to the final marvel of death and resurrection. Christ and Moses also were magicians.

All this is contradictory and confusing, and does not at all explain why we are in general so fascinated with magic in its many different forms. We all love magic; we all (even those who scoff the loudest) believe in some aspect of it. How many people saw Rosemary's Baby or The Exorcist? How many read Castaneda? How many (many more than you think, and from all over the world) attended a sorcerer's conference in Bogotá? How is it to be sorted out, and how is our own involvement with it to be understood ?

The idea of magic as gnosis, religion's method and technique, which is heartless without religion just as religion is powerless without magic, suggests a way in which many doubts could leave their uneasy circling to take a new and developing direction, uncovering new questions. What is the difference between tradition and traditionalism? Does a teaching cease to live when it becomes a dogma and is no longer a search to realize the master's method as well as understand his meaning? Can a teaching, then, long survive the teacher, or how is it renewed when the teacher is gone? What is a master or a teacher, and what are the signs of a true one?

DEATH

In the twilight of an era, as in the twilight of an individual life, one's thoughts turn more and more to the dark ending and the doubtful question of another sunrise. We may be either morbidly obsessed with death or searching for its meaning, and this meaning surely conditions, orients, limits to the finite, or expands to the infinite the meaning of our life. Even if we choose the quest for meaning, it would be absurd to think that one could do more than open some new questions; but this is perhaps not unimportant.

When we search the scriptures, we find among them, again, traces of a sort of home base, hints of a common ground in a knowledge of the human and cosmic facts: facts which are hidden in mystery for the literalism of the intellect, and so an eternal source of argument and difference; yet the knowing of those facts is there present in the very marrow of our bones and flows in our bloodstream. The mind (or what we call the mind) cannot see beyond the logic of the opposing and mutually exclusive poles, the two ends of the line: life and death, good and bad, yes and no. It is only when the more organic perceptions join the mental vision that the "line" is seen for what it is: one surface of a many-dimensional whole. Then the sterile impasse of the two is released into a creative, moving combination of three opening to four and five and the possibilities of infinity. Then we see that the "opposites" are not opposites at all, but steps of a process, and that difference does not mean contradiction. In place of the sentimental, literary concept of life as waking and death as sleep, we find suggestions in every teaching that on the contrary, death is waking, "from the dream of having lived." In the Tibetan Buddhist teaching, death is never considered to be the antithesis of life, but the correlative of birth; birth, life, and death form the moving triad which opens to another and another in new reincarnations.

Everywhere in the sacred texts and in the most authoritative commentaries we find our understanding shaken out of its one-planed dualism and offered the lifting perspective of an infinite range of levels. "Body" and "soul" become a process of bodies and souls in an ever-expanding view. Sheikh Ahmad Ahsa'i has delineated a structure of four bodies through which the "I-spirit" passes as upon stepping stones to its immortal perfection. The Zohar tells us of three aspects of the soul "each with its separate abode," but with the possibility of final union. The Egyptian Book of the Dead refers to khat, the physical body, and sahu, the spiritual body, and in the Epistle to the Corinthians, St. Paul speaks openly of the secret teaching, only hinted at elsewhere in Christian scripture, of the perfecting process of incarnation of the spirit in other bodies. Must there perhaps be an incarnation in this life before there can be reincarnation? What part does the human will, human intention and effort, play in this process—or none at all? Is something up to us?

So in our search through the traditions, we discover questions and also see glimpses of a common ocean floor from which it would seem that all the apparently separate islands of belief arise, and in which, for all their superimposed discrepancies, they are secretly joined.

CREATION

I f the door through which we pass out of this life is mysterious, equally so is the door by which we enter it. Though we have all come through it—and those who believe in reincarnation say that we have passed both doors countless time—that part of consciousness which we call memory cannot contain the experience. Our coming is as unknown to us as our going. What was our beginning? We never know and are always looking, because where we came from, and how, and why, conditions our present situation as the present determines the future. Our lives make sense only if they have an aim, if they follow a direction from their beginning toward their end. We need to know the starting point; we cannot be, like Danny Kaye's song, a-story-that-begins-in-the-middle-for-the-benefit-of-those-who-came-in-in-the-middle. Our stories about ourselves and the world reach back for that starting point: "Once upon a time..." — "In the beginning..."

> "In the beginning God created the heaven and the earth...And God said, Let us make man in our image, after our likeness..."

Every race, every people has a story of their beginning. There are countless creation myths, differing widely in the imagery of their description, yet with a recurrent idea of many levels of existence: of patterns repeated in different worlds in shifting forms. The laws of these patterns of repetition and the process of their transformation from level to level, from galaxy to snowflake, are a kind of cosmic mathematics. These laws are the structure of a continuing process, and the patterns they create are in movement; the repetition is not static but alive in a continuous regeneration.

Genesis tells of the covenant the Creator made with His creation: "While the earth remaineth, seedtime and harvest, and cold and heat, and summer and winter, and day and night shall not cease." The pattern of cycles, the rhythm of alternation and renewal, the rise and fall of the seasons and of human breath, the reflecting patterns of molecule and planet, seem to show enormous, interlocking relationships; what appears is a cosmic ecological system. What then is the use and function of the human being? We were made to nourish God, according to the Popol Vuh; in the view of the Dogon, we are a resonance, a vibration of the creating sound, that in its turn, on its smaller scale, creates. In the Zoroastrian myth of Asha, the human being is the balancing force between light and darkness, between good and evil. Genesis says that we are the image of God, made to reflect and echo the Ruler of all things in our own little world, as a kind of surrogate ruler and creator. And in every civilization that has remembered its mythic beginnings and acknowledged its origin in a higher level, the "creation" the human is capable of, in art, in craft, in every manual work and manifestation, is considered a service or help to the divine.

From this point of view, human creation is an imitation, a reflection of the sacred, of the higher level, of another world or worlds of meaning. And either we must say that human creation is not only what we call art, or we must enlarge the concept of art to include all human manifestation, to admit the arts of relationship, of work, of living. With this meaning of the word we can better understand the saying of Coomaraswamy: "No man has a right to any social status who is not an artist."

So what is an artist? What do we "make," and what necessary (and to whom necessary?) substance or energy is generated by our making? These are big and important questions for the searcher for meaning, and for anyone who feels, with the psalmist, the need to pray that the Lord preserve our going out and our coming in.

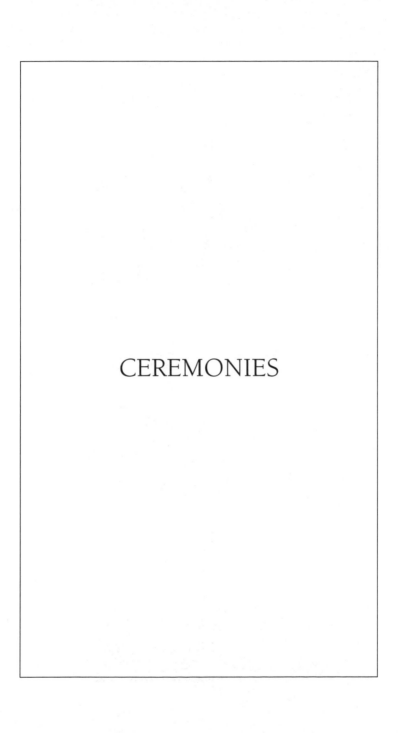

CEREMONIES

INITIATION

We are hearing a great deal these days about Kali yuga and the ending of our era. Fear is as heavy in the atmosphere we breathe as the fumes of our cars and factories; and although human beings have always lived in fear of death, in our times it seems that the race as a whole trembles for fear not only of death but of disintegration and total disappearance. Is this, then, any time to be talking about initiation, the mysterious rite which means beginning? How could we think about a new beginning when everything seems to be rushing towards dissolution?

But from another point of view, this is exactly the moment to be talking about it. For initiation only arrives at a beginning through an ending that makes a new growth possible. In the non-initiatic sense, what seem to be two sides of a contradiction are instead linked stages of a whole process: dissolution and death must precede a new birth. "Except a corn of wheat fall into the ground and die, it abideth alone; but, if it die, it bringeth forth much fruit."

A child (or an adult) must suffer the death of very dear illusions in order to come to another and truer relation with the divine. Ishtar must lose her jewels and her robe; a discipleship as it intensifies is stripped of words and symbols. Over and over, the initiation rites show us loss, sacrifice, suffering, and death as the road leading to the door into a transformed life. The moment of revelation, the new birth, has to be won; there is a whole process of training, an education and a discipline, that must prepare the candidate for that testing. When transformation is forgotten, the need to prepare for "that monumental jolt," in the words of don Juan, is forgotten also. In our day education has ceased to be a preparation for initiation; it has lost its true function of a training for inner maturity by a tempering of the will. Answers are given, information injected, instead of a channel opened to receive knowledge and an instrument prepared to re-express it.

The initiatic process of transformation is a journey of return: a "return to Paradise," to the original home for which some buried memory in the human being has always longed. "Initiation lies at the core of any genuine human life," Mircea Eliade has told us; for it is a re-entrance into creation, a going back to the regenerative source of power from which we came.

Here we have a hint of another aspect of initiation: as the process must begin long before the great moment of revelation and change, so it must continue afterward; it is the beginning of something; the new birth is for a new experience of living. And the next stage again is full of difficulty and trial, and perhaps eventual triumph; it leads to another ending, and so on like the ouroborus, the snake that swallows its own tail in an infinite circle—a continual going forth and a continual returning.

Is there a road of return for us to the house of our father? Can the prodigal come home? This country has always seemed proud of being an orphan, proud of its independence of its ancestors. Yet as Stephen of Hungary said, "without a past, a nation has no future"; and perhaps our present fear and uncertainty show that a two hundred-year history is not long enough to make a future we can feel sure of. Perhaps we begin to find that it is not so wonderful after all to be traditionless; perhaps we begin to look a little more humbly toward what was there before our beginnings. We need the power it could still transmit. It would be a comfort if we could look back far enough to glimpse a Wiracocha to point the way, to herald the birth of a new sun.

Yet whatever our unfaithfulness to them or our lack of respect, we have all had forefathers; no more than other people do we need to date our arrival on earth. The true past of this country (if not of this nation) is in the traditions of a people whose past is far longer than the one we claim. It is to the ancestors now of all our many tribes that we need to turn—not to try vainly to turn back the clock, not to imitate the past, but to change: to change "totally," into "beings who will never be the same again," in Eliade's words, having received the power to endure, the wisdom to know, and the weapons to slay the alien gods.

RITES OF PASSAGE

I t is significant that the word rite comes from the same root as art and order. Like all real art, like the movements of sacred dances, ritual provides order, a pattern, a channel through which the energy of an event or a series of events can flow in an evolutionary process toward a larger meaning, or a new stage or level of life. It offers us ways in which our transitions may be illuminated, helped to move up to consciousness instead of falling into accident and chaos: made to make sense. It is a ladder or a bridge, like that of the Noh theater's stage, marking the slow and exact steps of a passage from one world to another, between our ordinary daily lives and another dimension of meaning which surrounds us and yet is a "mystery" because our "eyes are closed" to it (mystery < muein, to close the eyes or mouth).

But the bridge itself is not a mystery and the eyes must not be closed. This passage has strict requirements. What combination of long discipline and inspiration, what marriage of service and grace, produces the Noh actor, or indeed any real artist? The hero may be you or me, but only at the highest reaches of our most impossible possibility. The Symplegades were never traversed by accident or in a dream, but only in the most active instant of a perfect and present attention. The rite of passage demands our total participation.

What happens, then, when there is no such participation? For it is not that we can choose to approach myth and ritual consciously or not at all; we have no choice, we cannot escape them. We live in them, as P.L. Travers has said, as an egg yolk in its albumen. If we are not related to them consciously and intentionally, then perforce our involvement is unconscious and accidental. And as myth and ritual are "magic" of a very high potency, accidental involvement is as dangerous as wandering absent-mindedly between the Clashing Rocks.

What have we done to our rites, and what are they doing to us? How rarely, among us, is a person's death that Rite of Passage charted in the Tibetan Book of the Dead? How much more commonly do we agree to participate in the terrible clinical ritual of tubes, drugs, and needles, followed by the lugubrious ceremonies of the "funeral parlor." Unrecognized rituals, molding our political life, push its processes further and further from our real needs and bring out, instead of considered judgment, all our tribal atavisms. Even the recognized rituals of our religious and civil celebrations have become at best "superstitions," for nothing "stands out" or remains of their real meaning but the outer forms. The Easter bunny has replaced the risen Christ; Christmas, extraordinary symbol of the birth of a possibility, has become first and foremost a frantic shopping spree, and Thanksgiving a day of overindulgence rather than of gratitude and re-evaluation.

All that can save us is to return to the underlying meaning, to turn to myth and symbol in the spirit of quest: like don Juan's warrior, looking, trying only to see, knowing ourselves on the brink of doom but not doubting our character of potential hero: "wide awake, with fear, with respect, and with absolute confidence."

A great Lakota medicine man said: "There is a place where the impossible becomes possible. But one must see and fully trust." And this means facing oneself as mercilessly as Quetzalcoatl and taking a risk as great as Jason's.

SACRIFICE

In 1971, I had the good fortune to be invited by a Lakota friend to a celebration of the Sun Dance. It was a serious event, not for tourists; there were police to turn away unauthorized persons. It was an unexpected mixture of old and new. People came in cars instead of (as it seemed they should) on horseback; a loudspeaker blared between chants of ritual songs. Here was no relic of the past preserved under glass; it was the old way, not quite the same but very much alive in modern dress. Over the loudspeaker, in English and Lakota: Would the woman who was menstruating please leave at once? Her presence was having a harmful effect on the dancers... There could be no doubt that everything in that charged atmosphere was shared by everyone. We, the onlookers in the brush shelter that circled the dancing space around the sacred tree, were also participants. When there was a weakening in the shrilling whistles and the hard beat of the dancers' feet under the pressure of the fierce sun, we danced behind them in the circle of branches to lend them strength. The medicine men cared for them constantly, dancing with them, gazing with them at the sun, brushing them with their eagle-wing fans to draw away weakness and touch them with the eagle's soaring power. When the young men offered their flesh to the knife and the thong, the trilling of the women sent joy and sorrow and triumph to meet each conquest of pain; the drums and chanting vibrated their exchange of energy. Nothing was explained; but I would never again need a definition of sacrifice.

OBSTACLES

Obstacles. We spend our lives fighting them, over-
coming them, getting around them, or making excuses for being stopped by them. How much of all this
energy is spent tilting at windmills? Something, certainly,
stops us from attaining what we wish and being what we
could be; but is it what—or where—we think it is?

Opposition and challenge from the outside evident-
ly stimulate us to do battle, exercise and train us, develop
our muscles and our patience. They play Marpa to our
Milarepa, if there is any Milarepa in us at all. They help rather
than hinder. But there is something inside everyone that
resists help—a coward shadow that dogs the heels of our
potential hero. This is the real obstacle, and it is very close
to home; we have met the enemy, as Pogo says, and he is
us.

For many years I have been drawn to the question and
the extraordinary potential of obstacles. Hindrance and possibility, force and resistance, I cannot and I would, are what
we are made of, from little boys and little girls to big ones.
And the capacity to reconcile that inner conflict—over and
over again, perhaps, in a gradual process of creating a more
mature and balanced whole—is the exclusively human char-
acteristic; it is what differentiates us from the animals. We
know in our bones that the final glory, the ultimate
achievement, of the human being is to master himself. This
does not have to mean that he is successful in "overcom-

ing" all those outer barriers, nor that he becomes a saint who eliminates every trace of the natural mortal. One who masters himself is in charge of what he is. He has brought about a relation between the animal and the divine in him, through which the animal is cared for and the divine is served. And this means, sometimes, the apparent absence of struggle: the huge, often invisible effort of acceptance of what one cannot change. No aspect of the battle for self-mastery is harder than this one of renouncing one's natural "rights" and desires, to find what lies beyond them, an inner peace. For when the higher will conquers the lower, the result appears to be a joyful freedom from both victory and defeat. "To be victorious and to be defeated are equal," says don Juan. "Everything is filled to the brim and everything is equal and my struggle was worth my while."

Such freedom must be costly and painful to acquire, and we put off the attempt to gain it as long as possible—usually until it is too late. But we know it is our real destiny, and that we are capable of achieving it. ("You could free me if you would," says the enchanted princess to the man in the fairy tale.) And when we are aware of someone else engaged in this struggle, we recognize it with a kind of leap of the heart. Another person fights our battle with us and for us; we are allies.

No matter how bravely one may face the outer foe, the true nobility of the warrior is in how he faces himself. Any animal will fight for its physical life and need, but only a human being can fight for his soul.

CEREMONIES

The word ceremony comes from a Latin word which means "sacredness." Isn't it strange that in our irreligious times, possibly the furthest removed in history from a relation with the sacred, ceremonial forms should be so great a part of our profane lives? Look at the New York parades on any holiday; the ritual pomp of football games with their bands and drum majorettes; the panoply of Lodge initiations. Graduation ceremonies begin now in kindergarten, with our five-year-olds in caps and gowns.

We take our passion for rituals for granted; we may question their forms, but never the need for their existence. But why this apparently growing need? We no longer acknowledge the thirst for a relation with another level, the thirst to which our religions sought ritually to minister; nevertheless, however deeply buried, it continues to exist. Are we unconsciously trying to allay it with the empty cup of our mostly meaningless rites?

It seems that what is genuine in our need to solemnify, celebrate, ritualize the things that happen in our lives originates in something as basic as the incompleteness of our being. For we see that a person—or a community—usually seeks a ceremony at the moment of recognizing human inadequacy in the face of life events. At a moment of sudden danger, even a total unbeliever prays. When help is needed for a difficult transition, or a blessing on an achievement or a new possibility, one feels the insufficiency of one's own force, even to be a successful petitioner. A person is too small, and that which can help and bless is too great. Perhaps one could say that the real need for a ceremony arises in the moment when we recognize our place.

In that place we are humble; we need an intercessor, we look for someone closer to the throne than we are, a priest or a shaman, to plead for us; and we need others to plead with us. Even "private" ceremonies must be performed in a limited public of family and friends. Those gathered to celebrate the rite cannot be "audience" or mere spectators; they have an active part to play in calling down the gift from above. And the ancient forms of the rituals, handed down through centuries, are also carriers of force, in the same way that the walls of old churches are impregnated with the power of the prayers they have absorbed.

All this, of course, refers to real ceremonies and to the conditions in which they can be effective. Any of them can become a rite of passage: an intercessory movement opening a channel between the human level and the sacred, through which the help and the blessing may come. But the truly sacred must be truly invoked. The difficulty—one can say, even, the danger—of our attempts to approach the throne consists both in how we approach, and in what is enthroned. It has been said that the problem of prayer is not that it is not answered, but that it is; and there are hungry ghosts hovering over our altars as well as bodhisattvas. Real help, real blessing, can come only when what is real in the human reaches for the highest in himself and something higher than himself. If it is not this that is invoked, the form of the invocation is a "vain repetition," or a social occasion, or an ego trip, or perhaps even black magic.

The ceremony is a reminder of our possible relation

with the sacred, and no ceremony can do more than help the celebrants to remember themselves in all their possible dimensions. But this is quite enough; indeed, it is all the help and all the blessing that could be asked. For a relationship re-membered is revitalized, brought to life, like Osiris delivered from Seth the Divider. Then giving and receiving become one, as the words were once in the original Indo-European root (ghabh). We call a religious ceremony a "divine service" without thinking that perhaps the title means literally what it says. People closer to life sources than we are, the Native Americans for instance, understand this and know that their ceremonies are needed by nature and by the earth their mother, by the Creator as well as by themselves.

Perhaps it is this almost forgotten element of service, this sense of exchange with the holy Whole, that is the greatest lack in our attempts at ceremony today.

PILGRIMAGE

U nder one form or another, we are always talking about the Way from here to there: the dangerous passage, the ladder of heroic ascent, the process of human completion—the transforming journey, for which still another name is pilgrimage.

Whatever aspect of the perennial question we apply ourselves to, we find new things to think about; we begin to see the differences in journeys, inner and outer. Certainly not all of them are pilgrimages. "Pilgrims," says Richard Niebuhr, "are persons in motion, passing through territories not their own, seeking something we might call completion, or perhaps the word clarity will do as well: a goal to which only the spirit's compass points the way."

Some journeys have no such compass and become simply sight-seeing tours. Others that we know of seem to be flights, and we go not from here to there but to some accidental pseudo-refuge, where conditions may be better, or perhaps the same or worse than ever. But even with the courage and the longing for inner change of the true pilgrim, the way can be lost if there is no guide; it can disappear completely, or it may turn out to be impassable, or lead in the wrong direction.

The guides have many shapes and forms. The Russian Pilgrim had his Philokalia, Dante his Virgil. In Journey to the East, besides the porter Leo there is the impetus of the quest itself. Herman Hesse wrote: "I realized that I had joined a pilgrimage to the East, seemingly a definite and single pilgrimage—but in reality, in its broadest sense, this expedition to the East was not only mine and now; this procession of believers and disciples had always and incessantly been moving towards the East, towards the Home of Light. Throughout the centuries it had been on the way, towards light and wonder, and each member, each group, indeed our whole host and its great pilgrimage, was only a wave in the eternal stream of human beings, of the eternal strivings of the human spirit towards the East, towards Home." But even so joyfully accompanied, "H.H." loses both his way and its unrecognized leader; dazzled by the glory of the adventure, he cannot see himself, and he has a long inner pilgrimage to make through loss and suffering before he learns to find the way again and to recognize the guide.

For we cannot, it seems, find the way alone. Whether guidance comes from the servant Leo, ancient custom, or an image of the Holy Grail itself, we must know for sure that "the spirit's compass" points in the same direction. The teaching of the Ways is in the terms of myth, which does not necessarily end with being happy ever after. What is needed for the journey towards completion, besides a Way and a guide, courage and desire, seems to be both luck and good judgment, and a good deal of both. For only by unusual good fortune are the conditions found, and the best conditions fail if they are not seen and understood; and nothing about the Way is guaranteed. The facts that it exists and there are guides, that the traveler is free to choose and can be sure that prayer is answered, make it all the more dangerously necessary that he or she see very clearly indeed how to choose and what to ask for.

This is not to say that the pilgrim's choice to be "a person in motion" is unwise. Stay-at-homes don't appear to be taking so great a risk only because their fates move toward them on accustomed paths, more slowly if more certainly; bed, it has been said, is the most dangerous place in the world, for more people die there than anywhere else. Perhaps rather than choosing, the pilgrim is chosen by his or her own way of being. What is important, finally, is to be in motion. Guide and goal, vital as they are to the journey, are secondary to the journey itself which is the most important thing of all. Whoever feels this can say with don Juan: "For me there is only the traveling on paths that have heart; there I travel, looking, looking, breathlessly."

THE TWO AND THE ONE

RELATIONSHIPS

I t seems a very strange thing that of all the forms of life on this planet, the human being—the most intelligent, the most powerful, the most capable of controlling its environment and so of relative independence—is also the form of life which has the longest period of physical dependence and immaturity. No other creature has so evident and so prolonged a need for its parents; on no other creature is the lesson of family and of relationship so deeply impressed by its own necessities.

Is that why we rebel? For rebellion against parents and family seems an inevitable part of our experience. The generation gap was not invented in modern times; the Old Testament, paradigm of patriarchal tradition, is full of stories of disobedient sons and quarreling brothers. Is that a part of the lesson, perhaps? Must we first resist our human bonds in order to learn to accept them; run away from home so as to come back, like the prodigal, knowing ourselves better?

For certainly we can only begin to become aware of our own identity in terms of where it belongs and its place in the whole of what surrounds us. We know nothing, in fact, and can learn nothing, except by means of contact and comparison with other things and other people. The family is only the beginning of our education in rubbing elbows with the world, but as such it forms the basis for all our future participations. If we refuse, and continue to refuse, this first training in relationships, we have little prospect of success with other, even more difficult ones; and however much we may at times resent our human interconnectedness, we must also admit that most if not all of the joy, color, and warmth of our lives comes through contact with other people.

Beyond the family we were born into, based on the family, come all the other exchanges with friends and lovers, teachers, masters, dependents, husband and wife, son and daughter. And beyond all these is all of life in all its forms and manifestations, for what is there that is not in relation with something else? And below them, within them, conditioning them all, taught and formed by them all, is the relation with oneself, and the possible return to one's own deepest sources.

All this, if we obey the rules. But if we were not the inventors of the generation gap, we take it and its accompanying and continuing tantrums as seriously as if we were. We indulge its kicking against the pricks by yielding to all sorts of pretenses that things are not the way they are. We pretend that there are no differences between the sexes except a small biological one (vive la petite différence), call our parents by their first names to make them the same age as ourselves, and encourage every individual (but if we are all as alike as peas in a pod, what is an individual?) to do his or her own thing. We will have equality, even if our brand of it eliminates all real liberty and all real fraternity. But appeasement, we should have learned, brings its own perils. Rebellion there may and perhaps must be in order to come to maturity, but maturity must come, with the capacity and the insight to accept the facts of the human condition. We are learning to our cost that our apparent domination of our planet, and possibly others, does not make us free to do as we please with it. Other forms of life that we consider subject to our will, as well as and including our own, can still punish and perhaps destroy us utterly for our transgressions against a natural order.

We are all caught in Indra's net, in which, the myth tells us, at every crossing of the strands a bell is attached, so that any single movement, be it ever so slight, sets the whole in motion and every bell to ringing. Is it cacophony, or harmony? Does it depend on how we move and how we hear? Is this interweaving of relationships a cruel doom, or the possibility of treasure multiplied? Can we know before the final bell rings for our apparent exit?

"No man is an island," wrote John Donne, "sufficient unto himself; every man is a piece of the continent, a part of the main; and if a clod be washed away by the sea, Europe is the less, as if a promontory were, as if a manor of thine own or thy friend's were. Every man's death diminisheth me, for I am a part of mankind; therefore send not to know for whom the bell tolls: it tolls for thee."

ANDROGYNY

The search for meaning begins with a wish to deepen our own understanding of our own selves. But at the very outset of the journey inwards, there is a crossroads. Signs point in both directions, and I am pulled both ways. I find that I am double. I want something and at the same time I don't want it; I love and hate the same person. I am light and dark; I aspire to the heights and love my comfort. What it the meaning of this built-in contradiction, and what can my meaning be in the face of it?

The inherent duality of being has been expressed perhaps since time began by the symbol of the Androgyne: the two-in-one, the perfect being which accepts, includes, and reconciles its opposites. The conundrum is expressed with the greatest succinctness in Poimandres: "Beyond all creatures, man is twofold... Though male-female, as from a father male-female, and though he is sleepless from a sleepless sire, yet is he overcome by sleep." Sleep and waking: the greatest contradiction in the paradoxical being of humankind.

Yet it is our being; we did not choose it, we are so made. We are able to struggle to be masters of our sleep, not to be "overcome" by it, but we will never overcome it either. The opposites are there by divine decree. Where, then, is the hope of unity and of reconciliation, and of meaning in that sense of singleness and wholeness?

Curiously enough, the divine decree, as expressed in

Genesis, is couched like a promise rather than a penalty. "I will not again curse the ground, neither will I again smite any more every thing living; while the earth remaineth, seed-time and harvest, and cold and heat, and summer and winter, and day and night shall not cease." The meaning, the unity, the whole circle is there in the movement of this polarization. How to keep the wholeness, how not to lose summer in the avoidance of winter? Wanting unity and having duality, we try to solve the problem by eliminating one of the two, or be pretending they are both the same. But the reconciliation of male and female is not through uni-sex. The child, the third, the new one, comes from the union of opposites, not the adding of two like numbers or the subtraction of one of them. Our notion of solving the problem is to avoid the confrontation, and this is against Nature's law, as she is constantly showing us. The struggle which we want so much to avoid seems to be inevitable, and is in fact the process by which meaning becomes clear.

As for the duality of ourselves, of our very being—"mortal because of body, but immortal because of the essential man"—no choice is permitted, nor are we ever able, in this life, to know the outcome. Perhaps after all we have to accept that our meaning is contingent on something far beyond us, that we "make sense" only as part of a process. What we bring to the process may be just the energy of the struggle between the eternal two in us.

THE CHILD

What is childhood? Is it a privileged period of life up to a certain age, or is it the beginning of a trajectory that to all human intents and purposes may be as "eternal" as the life processes of stars and planets? As the beginning of the human life process, how far can it go? What is the ultimate possibility of man and woman? Can anything continue to develop after the death of the body, and if so, what could it eventually become? Would we, like lead, "become gold if we had time"? And how much does any of this depend on how the process begins?

Questioned in this way, the meaning and importance of childhood take on a sense of dependence on the meaning and importance of the process that it opens—the process of creation itself. And little as we appear to recognize that, much as we sentimentalize about children and childhood per se, something in us is essentially aware of it, for we really don't wish children to remain children. Even at their smallest and most enchanting, we rejoice quite naturally at each new sign of change toward maturity: the new tooth, the first step, the beginning words. When a child dies in infancy, the loss is unbearably tragic, yet we feel no grief at all at losing a child just as completely as he or she grows up. Something in us knows that it is more to be an adult than a child.

But this is not so, of course, if the growing is not truly up into another level of understanding and capacity—if it is not a real maturity in other than physical ways. If, as has been said, the only difference between men and boys is the size of their toys, then the "more" of the adult over the child is one of mere volume. Too many of us are only larger and dirtier children; but we complain bitterly when our children "grow up" to be basically the same as the rest of us. What can change, what must change for the process of evolution to continue? Or perhaps I should say, for it to take place; for we talk about "evolution" and "progress" in the blithest possible way, as if it were something that was bound to go on by itself and that we had no evident responsibility in the matter.

This loss of responsibility to a life process—and consequently, of course (although we would deny it indignantly), to our own children—is something our times have to answer for. I believe that its direct cause is the prior loss, by our preceding generations, of the recognition of levels—levels of being, and their consequent meanings and manifestations, which are wholly different in kind and in dimensionality one from another. Everyone thinks they grasp the idea of levels, but that few do is proved by our goals and our way of living. And without it, all our processes are linear, all our discoveries are simply rearrangements of what was already there. But in the light of this idea, we see ourselves as links in a great, vertical, life-bearing and possibly life-transforming chain, and we cannot avoid our responsibility.

We have played with our large toys in such a way that we are leaving our children a badly messed-up world. And we seem to be teaching them to go on playing the same games with even bigger playthings. It is not the playthings that are to blame; technology is not in itself an evil. It is the way of taking it as something to play with that is an attitude of childhood that should be left behind, and replaced with an adult understanding of tools to serve a responsible purpose.

It is greatly to be hoped that we can mature enough to learn this before it is too late to help our children.

STORYTELLING AND
EDUCATION

Anyone who has been in the presence of His Holiness the Dalai Lama would wish for oneself or one's own child even a part of the qualities he manifests; anyone would wish to have and to be able to pass on the wisdom and compassion that he urges on us. "Do I sound unrealistic?" he asks, laughing. Indeed, how are wisdom and compassion possible? Can these things be passed on, taught? Are they the result of education? What is education?

We know that life has produced great knowledge and great men and women; we recognize that most of what we know has come to us from other people. Since time's beginning the oral tradition—the great process of the transmission of knowledge-energy from one person or one generation to another—has found its expression in stories: stories enacted in rituals, represented in art, narrated and sung in myth and poetry, and written down in books. The word that is said can be put on paper, and I believe that the written word not only need not betray the spoken one, but may be its very loyal servant. The scriptures also are holy. What is vital is that what is written should indeed be an echo of lived truth, and not only a description.

Education in our times cannot take place without the written word; but it cannot take place either, in our times or any other, without the spoken one, without the voice of the teacher. Perhaps in the relation between the two is the very essence of transmission. In the beginning was the word, and word has to be incarnated in a form that can preserve the soul, the echo of that original vibration. Alas for the words, or the art, or the ritual, that forget their origin and their purely secondary function of expressing it, and begin to strut like the louse in the Popol Vuh, in love with their own importance. And alas for us, if we let ourselves be fooled into thinking that the expressions, the tools and instruments of teaching and learning, can be themselves the teachers. There is no substitute for the teacher and the teacher's voice: for the story told aloud, for the scripture read aloud, for the living gesture that interprets human understanding. Knowledge may be expressed in many forms, but someone must express it and someone else receive it, test it, and interpret it anew. Whatever education is or is not, it must be the transmission of a living energy, and human beings must exchange it.

For if we cannot define education, we surely can see some elements that are vital to it, and begin to demand that they should not be lacking in our schools. Education, which means a leading out, must mean a development from the inside, an opening of the inner eye; it must mean a development of inner strength. The word "discipline" is out of style, but it simply means teaching, and the learning of the teaching by a "disciple." And if the truth makes us free, true education surely also must bring a kind of inner liberation from our more ignorant inner slaveries—especially, as Krishnamurti says, freedom from fear.

What H.H. the Dalai Lama has shown us in his own person is an educated man. Perhaps it is only people who are educated in this sense who can respond to life, its situations and inhabitants, its exiles and its thrones, with what he calls wisdom and compassion.

MUSIC, SOUND, AND SILENCE

What is sound, and is silence only its absence? What is the relation between music and sound and noise? What does music include, or exclude? What does it do, what is it for?

These questions are not answered; although there are replies, some of them charming like the child's "Music is the house sound lives in"—but is it really more than a child's definition? Are any of our answers more than children's definitions?

When I look to the myths, which never define and always throw light, I am struck by the fact that over and over again, stories of the world's beginning ascribe it to a sound, a creative vibration, a breath, a word, or a song. "In the beginning was the Word"; and the Kathapada Upanishad says that "everything the gods do, it is by chanting that it is done." Here is the account of the creation in the Popol Vuh:

> There was nothing brought together, nothing which could make a noise, nor anything which might move, or tremble... Nothing existed. There was only immobility and silence in the darkness, in the night... Then came the word... "Earth!" they said, and instantly it was made.

The notion of music, seen from the concept of sound as the life force, becomes huge; but somehow we assent to it. It "strikes a chord," and the very expression witnesses its truth; as P.L. Travers would say, it is in our bloodstream. Our questions are too small, it seems, to be answered; music is indefinable because it is a movement toward something larger than our vision—creation itself, a structure of universal order whose top vanishes in the clouds. The composer Steve Reich has written that "listening to an extremely gradual musical process opens my ears to it, and it always extends farther than I can hear."

I think it was Aldous Huxley (or was he quoting someone?) who said, "There is only one noun; and all the verbs are ways of reaching it." I think music has to be taken as a verb—an action, a movement-towards; continually changing, searching, reaching, sometimes unquestionably touching some enormous paradigm and striking a bell that sets all our inner tuning-forks to ringing. When this happens, is something ordered in the hearer, is a connection made with another energy which for a moment at least makes us whole? "Music helps keep us in touch with the whole vibrating world," Yehudi Menuhin writes in The Music of Man, "and thereby centers us in our own being."

So the nearest we have come to a definition is no definition at all, but the vague sense that music has to do with an inner relation. Great music puts us in order; it makes things make sense. Listening, we feel a kind of relief: ah yes! that is it! We recognize another world, and we are here contained in this one, and know our place between the two. It is the loss of this relation that makes our lives senseless, for if there is no level higher than ours, no will or consciousness beyond the human, no "heaven" above us, then there is no earth beneath us either. This is just where we find (or lose) ourselves today, having refused both sonship and stewardship; having renounced our vital dependence on the sacred, we have of course lost all sense of responsibility toward the earth and the forms of life that depend on us. But what the laws of music and vibration reveal is precisely this structure in which we can find our roots and our reason for being, all the more convincingly because the vision is reflected in all other aspects of existence as in an infinite series of mirrors. The vibrant sound which is the life force is also movement and heat and color. The law of the octave echoes through the light spectrum and through the cycles of every human life.

If music, as we have been told, is organized sound, is it indeed the musician, the ordinary human being, who organizes it? Or does he discover, if he is very lucky as well as very disciplined, the laws to which it miraculously corresponds?

MASK AND METAPHOR

One of my favorite Mullah Nasr Eddin stories tells how the Mullah went to the bazaar to buy cloth. Finding all the booths of the cloth merchants full of customers bidding and driving up the prices, he stationed himself near the opposite end of the bazaar and began shouting at the top of his lungs about the bargains there, hoping to draw away his competitors. He was so successful that people started streaming down to that end of the bazaar, leaving the cloth sellers' booths empty for him, just as he wished. But seeing all the people hurrying by, he thought: Perhaps there really are splendid bargains down there! So he abandoned the cloth dealers and ran after the crowd.

This story pokes wonderful fun at the tricky and self-serving person who falls into his own trap. But if we don't just dismiss it as a good joke on such people (the others), it could throw a useful light on how we all play the roles and wear the masks that are a legitimate and necessary part of our human lives. For some unseen director gives us roles to play, whether we wish it or not, haphazardly or for some purpose we can't be sure of. We are born, as it were, on stage, in the middle of a play we didn't write. To what extent, then, can we act? Do we play the parts assigned to us, or do they play us? What have we to say about them? Almost nothing, certainly, as long as we, like the mullah, are fooled by them; as long as we believe we are those characters. And we have a terrible tendency to believe in appearances. We are played by our roles as long as they are more real for us than our own unseen reality. The masked and costumed character is visible and we confuse, it seems, the mask and the costume with the person behind them; we take the role for the player. But the actor is not Hamlet—or is he, and in what sense? It's true that if he doesn't become Hamlet—think, feel, speak as Hamlet himself—he fails in the part. But no matter how brilliantly he succeeds, he is never HAMLET; nor does he need to be, nor do we expect it of him. Yet we expect our fathers to be FATHER; or (perhaps worse) we reduce FATHER to our father's performance, or to our own when our turn comes to be cast in that part.

What would it mean to wear a mask consciously, to play an intentional role? Wouldn't it first of all imply seeing the difference between it and my own persona?—and like the Balinese mask player, trying to conform myself to it, never forgetting that the mask, as prototype, is greater than my person or any one person, and I can only strive to fill the aspect of it that I see, which is never (and cannot be) the whole.

Have I a "real" face, or are there only layers of the persona—mask after mask? Yet something is behind all this: a moving force, an actor, that could perhaps wear any face, or all of them. Perhaps, if this force were conscious, the masks, the roles, would be simply channels, through which it could express itself and whatever greater force it may spring from that may flow through it. If that were so, the mask would be a metaphor, a symbol, and a tool for the real self. And the real self might be itself a mask—a symbol and a tool for the life that is behind and above it. Perhaps this is an approach to the real meaning of the face within the face.

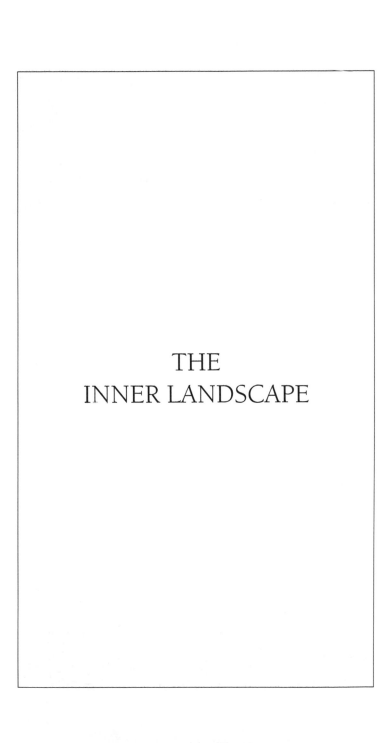

THE
INNER LANDSCAPE

DREAMS AND SEEING

The dream world is the greatest of all mysteries, the very home of mystery: that shadow land between where we are and where something in us came from, east of the sun, west of the moon, out of which come voices of poetry and myth, voices with messages. . . . Who sends these messages—angel, demon, or clown? What are the sources of our sleeping and waking dreams? Why are their messages so different, some so confused and some so clear?

> Sleep has two gates, they say: one is of horn
> And spirits of truth find easy exit there,
> The other is perfectly wrought of glistening ivory
> But from it the shades send false dreams up
> to the world. . .[1]

Virgil's well-known lines are almost a direct transcription from the Odyssey; and no doubt even long before Homer's day, the difference has been made between true dreams and false ones—hallucinations and visions, deception (or at best, nonsense) and revelation; dreams, as we say, that "mean something" or that "don't mean anything." But if we could understand, are there any dreams that don't mean anything, that send no message at all from anything to anyone? And are we sure we know the real difference between true and false? The word "myth," for instance, is often used to mean "lie," yet it is no lie, but as Coomaraswamy says, "the nearest to absolute truth that can be expressed in words."

Are there, then, different kinds or levels of truth? And what could be more vital than to know how to distinguish them from each other and from what opposes and denies them? It has been the business of the seeker, of the would-be hero and the warrior, from the very beginnings of myth and fairy tale, not to be fooled. But the difficulty is that truth and falsehood, delusion and revelation, are always mixed for us— like our sleep and waking.

How to discriminate? It means to know the mixture, the degree of sleep; to calculate the angle of distortion. Perhaps it is only the completely awakened person, the triumphant hero, who has gone beyond this duality; the hero's sight pierces delusion and has no need for flashes of revelation, since now the whole of reality is constantly before his eyes. But for us ordinary people, there are as many kinds of dreams as there are kinds and degrees of sleep, both physical and psychic. In physical sleep the rare phenomenon— one in thousands—is a dream that is all of a piece, without irrelevancies, and that has the authority of an important meaning; an undoubted message from a higher source, even if we can't at once decipher it and perhaps don't understand it fully until years later. Far more often, it is as if, at different times, different parts of us lose contact with the rest and become completely comatose, leaving only one or another fraction of us still experiencing and trying to express that experience in its own subjective code. At times the body is telling the story of its passing sensations; sometimes the emotions chatter about their fears and wishes; at others the head projects its anxious concerns—and all these in their own way and in varying proportions of mixture with each other and with sleep. And yet, perhaps each part is telling the truth as well as it can.

Much the same state of affairs prevails when we are physically awake, with the rapid and intermixing trains of associations that we call daydreams—although this intimate, secret part of our life is something we admit (or don't admit) that we indulge in, thereby claiming that we are, however, really in control of it. Are we, in fact, directing our daydreams, or are they also "bringing a message," a sort of seismograph of movements deeply buried in us? If we could follow the moving needle, might we see in this graph sketching our inner attractions and repulsions the outline of our unknown personalities?

If that is so, then beyond daydreaming it would seem there is a kind of dreaming that we have no word for, because we are mostly not aware that it exists: the delusion of ourselves, the amnesia of our real identity. And mixed in this hallucination of our life and of our world, there are glimpses of a different reality, a possible different landscape inhabited by different beings—flashes of vision that, perhaps, we take for dreams. And here our very lives depend on knowing ivory from horn.

1. Virgil, The Aeneid, Patric Dickinson, tr. (New York: A Mentor Book, New American Library, 1961), p. 145.

WHOLENESS

I t seems that willy-nilly everything follows a kind of circular process. There is no standing still, and no sudden transformation. The whole question, the only one to which our response is necessary, is whether the circles of our movement tend to become smaller or larger; whether they are closing down to a dwindling point, or opening to a greater and greater inclusiveness; whether or not, in other words, we are journeying toward wholeness. It is all a process, a journey toward; it can never be an arrival. Even our "wholeness" is relative—the measure of our capacity to measure the immeasurable.

Is the hero's victory the end of the quest, or the beginning of another, even more far-reaching? Does "happy ever after" mean eternal repose—or could happiness be the continuation of the process which brought the hero, only as a first step, to heroism? And can this process—never-ending, continually enlarging, forever changing—have any identifying signs?

This is not empty theorizing, for if we are to be the heroes of our own lives, this process claims us all; we work with it, or it devours us. And perhaps the identifying signs may be sought for (like the moon in its reflection in a puddle) in those, more accessible to us, of the anti-process, that which causes our fragmentation. For it is disintegration which we see as the central, terrifying fact of our personality-split, atom-split society—so central and so terrifying that even nuclear science begins to look for the moon's reflection.

In his book, Wholeness and the Implicate Order, an eminent physicist, David Bohm, says that in spite of the generally observable fact of fragmentation in human life, "wholeness is what is real," and fragmentation is only "the response of this whole to man's action, guided by illusory perception shaped by fragmentary thought." He defines it further as "in essence, a confusion around the question of difference and sameness (or oneness)... To be confused about what is different and what is not, is to be confused about everything."

Between the hurtful divisiveness of false differences and the waste of possibility in the "pudding" of a false sameness lies the entire hope of reality, of wholeness, and of relation. Through this "illusory perception shaped by fragmentary thought" we lose all chance of right relationship, which, as His Holiness the Dalai Lama has pointed out, is based on differences. And so we lose what might be our relative wholeness, since this can only be the wholeness of relating to and participating in a universe on another scale from our small selves.

If the first capacity of the hero is the capacity not to be fooled, we pray with St. Francis, "Lord, grant us the wisdom to know the differences." Yet, the wisdom is there, buried deep perhaps, but an integral part of our wholeness: the voice of conscience, the taste for the true, the recognition of the shape of the lie. It is there for our attention to find.

ATTENTION

Every tradition has a name for it—mindfulness, remembering, dhyana, kavanah, dhikr—and it is at the center of them all, for nothing can take place without it, except by accident. But no one has ever been able to define attention in its totality. We say it is this, it is that, and many of the things we say are true, but none of them is complete. Is it because it is so closely linked with being, which is equally indefinable? It has been said that "I am my attention." At any moment, its measure is the measure of what a person is, and it has as many characters, and degrees, and qualities, and levels as that greatest of all mysteries, the human being. It can be as absent, or as present, as the human soul; it can be as inconsistent, as weak, as enslaved as you or I at our most dispersed, or, if we listen to the great ones of any tradition, it can offer us something so high as to seem—were it not for a few rare, flashing memories and some undeniable intuition—quite inaccessible.

In spite of the different names, what is described in different teachings as the highest attention is quite clearly the same inner state. All agree that real, liberating attention cannot come exclusively from the mind as we are usually taught, but must be generated from feeling, and entered into with the body; it is an activity of the whole person, and closely allied with conscience.

In the wonderful collection of early Christian writings called the Philokalia, St. Simeon the New Theologian tells of "three methods of attention and prayer" for the serious seeker, but warns that only the third can lead him where he wishes to go. He writes:

> A true and straight path to the third method of attention and prayer is the following: The mind should be in the heart—a distinctive feature of the third method of prayer. It should guard the heart while it prays, revolve, remaining always within, and thence, from the depths of the heart, offer up prayers to God. . . .
>
> In a word, he who does not have attention in himself and does not guard his mind, cannot become pure in heart and so cannot see God. He who does not have attention in himself cannot be poor in spirit, cannot weep and be contrite, nor be gentle and meek, nor hunger and thirst after righteousness, nor be merciful, nor a peacemaker, nor suffer persecution for righteousness' sake. Speaking generally, it is impossible to acquire virtue in any other way except through this kind of attention. Therefore you should try to gain this more than anything else, so as to learn what I tell you in your own experience. . . . Keep your attention within yourself (not in your head but in your heart). Keep your mind there (in your heart), trying by every possible means to find the place where the heart is, in order that, having found it, your mind should constantly abide there. Wrestling thus, the mind will find the place of the heart. . . .[1]

Perhaps it is only our generation for whom it is a novel thought that the heart should "guard the mind" and "abide there," to bring about that state of right mindfulness, true attention, which is proper to the human being. Perhaps we have simply forgotten what has been known to the wise of past generations for millennia. "God demands only one thing from us," St. Simeon goes on to say, "that our heart be purified by means of attention."

1. From Writings from the Philokalia on Prayer of the Heart, E. Kadloubovsky and G.E.H. Palmer, trs. (London: Faber and Faber, Ltd., 1951).

TRIAD

One of the difficulties of thinking of the triad is the danger of being turned back by the limits of numbers—or rather, the apparent limits which the mind imposes on numbers when it separates them from each other and attempts to pen them up as individual concepts. But the magic of numbers, and their actual fluidity, is in their relationships and the interchanges between them. The triad is not three things that are similar or identical. It is the relation between quite different ones, for without difference there is no relationship. Unity begets diversity; one inevitably implies two, two calls for three, which becomes four—and so on to the octave and beyond.

Why then should we speak particularly of three? Perhaps because it signals the moment in the moving process of numbers when creation—we cannot say begins, because it is born in the one, but when it begins to manifest itself. We cannot see "relation" or "process" without the presence of the third, the unseen combining and evolving element. One brings forth its own two sides: male-female, plus-minus, for and against, the eternal contradiction which continues indefinitely in opposition until one side "wins," in which case nothing new happens; or until something else enters, a third thing—a new current or impulse which blends the opposites into a different, fourth entity. This is the process of creation, on all levels, physical and spiritual; we see its operation everywhere, and yet we never see it.

Is that because, or is it the result, of the fact that the human being is itself a triad? We are three-part beings: feeling, body, and mind, as indicated in the old symbol of the horse or team, the cart or chariot, and the driver. This is at once our structure and our possibility; for inasmuch as we are conscious, or potentially conscious, beings, we have an influence over the working of these parts, and it is that relationship of the three that can produce the unknown fourth that would be the true Self: the chariot's master and owner. Krishna would appear, and Arjuna, no longer confused and desperate, could stand up and fight.

So the triad is not about "the number three," but about relationships and reconciliation. "The three golden hairs" of the giant are not the triad which the story hints at; the three brothers, as P.L. Travers points out, are not three peas in a pod, distinguished only by their chronological order. The creative force of the triad seems to reside in its very difficulties, in the differences of its parts—and their possible reconciliation, never guaranteed. Yet we see the results of its action everywhere: in craft and architecture, in music, fairy tale, and the ways in which children learn; in the workings of our courts of law and in the smoking of the Native American pipe. The idea of divine trinity—so sadly neglected by the modern Church—seems to be part of the structure of the world's religions, even, as it were by default, in such a seemingly dualistic one as that of Zoroaster. Maybe it means something quite other, and much more pertinent to our lives, than our vague childhood notion of the Father, the Son, and Something Else.

God himself is a triad, and we three-part human beings are thus indeed created in his image. To see this law, then, as it works constantly in the natural world around us, is to see God. Perhaps to see it in ourselves is what we are here for. The Tao says:

> Heaven and earth would come together
> And gentle rain fall.
> Men would need no more instruction and all things
>   would take their course.

REPETITION AND RENEWAL

We are born to a cyclical world, to the repetition of change. We recognize this as a law of creation, and we accept quite willingly the recurrent patterns of Nature, even making up new patterns for ourselves and pursuing those made long ago by others. Our social customs, the way we eat and dress, conduct our businesses and our religious practices, all repeat the patterns we have invented or inherited. Why do we do this? We feel, as Peter Brook has said, that repetition is "like a force, which can have either positive or negative results." We do the same things over and over again, we say the same words, and to go through the same motions. When does this militate for renewal, and when for slow death? Is it a step forward (even our walking is a series of repeated steps), or does it work to erode the distance between levels and to go toward the leveling-off of a sort of psychological entropy? Does the repetition of the fathomless words of the Lord's Prayer deepen our understanding, or does it rattle away into a "patter" which owes its name, disgracefully, to that very prayer—the Pater Noster?

Mircea Eliade suggested that the law behind our adherence to patterns is, as it were, the law of our own evolution. There is a longing for a reality not wholly realized, a thirst for completed being, impelling human creatures to reach toward another world which the highest in them claims as home—a "nostalgia for Paradise" which makes them repeatedly strive to imitate whatever they know or feel or have heard of the sacred. Myths and symbols, rites and ceremonies were for ancient people (and perhaps they reverberate in the ancient core common to all people) "divine models" or "archetypes," or as Blake called them "Authors," when he spoke of myths: "The Authors are in Eternity." These are intimations of another, higher, larger world that our world can only imitate. Even the Nature of this world we live in seems to imitate something—as if seeking symbols to express a truth greater than ours; repeating over and over an effort that strives toward a perfection that is never attained.

Perhaps ancient people, being less in love than we are with mental forms and formulations, were more able to keep in touch with their own hunger for being, and so their search and its patterns remained alive. We are very little in touch with it, and even, at our peril, often deny its existence; so we have become expert at diverting its stirrings in us to exterior channels. We see repetition as necessary, not for imitation of the divine, but only for many things in our ordinary lives: for learning, for order and organization, for the mass production of things, as well as to preserve revered or useful relics of the past. But mostly, we find, repetition does not renew us; we yawn at our desks and daydream in our churches and our studios. We think of refreshment in terms of something "new," different, a change. But the change, the new, is latent in the very forms that have become stale for us because we know exactly (we think) what comes next and what to expect of the end result. Our error often is to see the patterns of our lives as things in themselves, which soon lose all their limited meaning and become closed circles. Then we are closed inside them with little space to move or air to breathe, and find ourselves in the stifling situations we know all too well in our daily lives and have so many words to describe. "Repetitious" means humdrum, monotonous, boring, deadly. But if we didn't delude ourselves that we knew all that these situations contain and exactly what would happen next, if the question were not lost, if the opening to the unknown were kept in sight (for it is always there), in this same routine there may be found a way of pursuing the expanding, ascending, endless spiral toward that other world that calls us because a part of us is already there. If the question is alive, repetition itself becomes change; and we experience what the Buddha said, that one "never steps twice into the same stream."

HOSPITALITY

D
o we ever take an idea seriously enough? Spending weeks with a predominating thought opens other avenues than those of the ordinary mind. One begins to experience the idea in action and to feel it in a new way. It makes its own surprising connections; one idea links itself with another, or perhaps with several. There seems to be an endless network of relationships in which every concept expands into a bewildering infinity; and what becomes clear is that we cannot take any word for granted and say that we understand it.

So we cannot take for granted the familiar word hospitality when we begin to see it in its rich context. Hospitality is a form of exchange, not a one-sided beneficence. The soup kitchen, though necessary, isn't in itself hospitality; maybe the lack of real hospitality in our day is the reason why people are homeless and soup kitchens exist. The exchange we speak of requires another level, and seems to correspond with a human need even deeper, and far harder to satisfy, than physical hunger. Its nature is a profound question.

To know that guest and host were once the same word, as were also give and receive, opens a window in the mind; yet another window opens when we look at the root meanings of please and thanks, those taken-for-granted words of our daily exchanges. But why should it please someone to give me what I ask for? What is the pleasure of the host?

And what does thank you mean? The English word, oddly enough, originally meant to think and to feel; the French word means mercy, and the Spanish, grace. Big ideas for such commonplace words! What do they imply? Can guest and host, if they understand their relation, share these wonderful gifts?

Certainly, in the largest sense, we are all guests—God's guests, if you like, guests of the earth, guests of life; but sometimes we are allowed for a moment to play the role of host to another human being, or to several; and what a caricature is made of it, unless it is seen as playacting (the model host would do well to remember the definition of "model" as "a small imitation of the real thing"). But perhaps if one can see oneself as an understudy, no different from one's fellow actor the guest, that right relationship may be arrived at, and both may have a sense of being partakers.

This exchange that we are searching for, however unconsciously, goes further than we habitually think. Our ideas of hospitality often leave out the higher element, the sacred "third" in the exchange to whom, as Lakota tradition tells us, the essence, the "juice" of the rite belongs. As all the traditional views of hospitality indicate, as well as all myths and fairy tales, the stranger, the unknown element, is the most important of all. Sometimes it hides itself in the role of the guest, as the god in disguise. Sometimes we are hosts to this mysterious guest, sometimes guests of a mysterious host—or perhaps we are always both. But it is in the mystery that the essential element is hidden; and if we scoff at mysteries, we do so at our peril. For without mystery, where is the question? And without the question, where are we?

TIME AND PRESENCE

As creatures dependent on time, we have to be concerned with it. But how to look at time? The more we grapple with it, the more it seems to change shape like the Old Man of the Sea. The one aspect offering a real contact with our living experience—and that too slips out of our grasp—is the present moment.

"Now" contains "all time, all the life" as Maurice Nicoll has proposed, yet, like a swinging trapeze, it eludes our grasp. The "active door" closes before we can pass through it, and in our search for the present moment in time, all we see is movement and change.

His Holiness the Dalai Lama says that it is not time that changes; rather, time is the measure of change. We experience it only in the shifting conditions in ourselves and our surroundings, in the course of the changeless rhythm of its movement. And mixed with these changes—real changes, such as growth and decay—are the changes in our reactions to them, much more varied, unpredictable, and less real although very convincing to us. The rhythm of time, the swinging cycles of nature, repeat themselves endlessly; if there are alterations in these cycles, they obey laws of such great magnitude that they are incomprehensible to us, even invisible. And in this pulsing, cyclical repetition seems to lie the secret of the unendingness of time, and the long successiveness of life on earth: the secret of rebirth, of renewal instead of death and decay.

Perhaps this successiveness of life is not guaranteed. Might it not have something to do with the relation of life on earth to time? It seems reasonable to suppose that there must be a harmony between their tempos, a sort of synchronicity, through which they support and reanimate each other. If this might be so, nothing could be more important than that exchange and interrelation; our problem would come from our effort to control time, to fight it instead of taking part in it.

What is it that has happened to our relation with time in the brief span of the past hundred years or even less—hardly an eye-wink in relation to the age of mankind and of the planet? Whence has come, and how has it taken such possession of us that we hardly notice or question it, the frantic need to do everything faster and faster? "Time-saving" devices, transportation at greater and greater speeds, fast food, instant gratification of all our appetites—we can't wait for the natural cycles, it takes too long for anything to mature at its own rhythm; and we don't question that, or wonder what will happen to us if we cut our contacts with these spirals of renewal, what horrible death by entropy awaits the human race, whose beginnings perhaps are even now visible.

We try to abolish time because our relationship with it has become simply one of fear. It is chasing us to destroy us, we seem to think; we must run, evade the pursuer; we must stay young, we must not allow old age to have any real place in our society, and we must not wait for anything but take quickly what we can get before it is too late. But if time is truly a dimension of human life and experience, what is it we are trying to abolish? What dimension of our humanity will disappear with it? How to accept the reality of the moment? How to see the facts, the actual forces at work, without running away into the past or the future?

Perhaps acceptance, the power to stay where one is without complaint or argument or imagination, is to move exactly in time with the ever-moving moment toward its fulfillment, toward the closing of the cycle: this privileged instant when the snake bites its tail, in the ancient symbol of the ouroboros, and so doing is immediately reborn into another circle of time renewed.

The present moment is one of power, of magic or miracle if we could ever be wholly in it and awake to it. As His Holiness has said, the "present" is impossible to find by logic of analysis. But it is not, as he himself exemplifies, impossible to live it. Not quite impossible perhaps, even for us, if we can hear the challenge of that astonishing "...an honor—a privilege—to live in these times."

SADNESS

D o we really know what sadness is? Many words and definitions spring to mind. But however closely they may be related, can we say that it is the same as grief, or despondency, or pain, or anguish, or sorrow, or depression? To call it un-happiness begs the question, for there are as many kinds of happiness as there are of sadness, and as many names for their different shades. It is not exactly the same to be joyful, elated, pleased, cheerful, fortunate, glad, or satisfied. Oddly enough, "satisfied" is one of the root meanings of the word "sad," which we think of as the antithesis of satisfaction or happiness. In Old English, saed means "sated"; Latin satis means "enough." So the original meaning of sadness is to have enough, or to have too much; yet the feeling of sadness in our human experience is connected with loss or lack. Has the content of the word changed so much that it has become its own opposite? Can words contradict themselves?

Here there is something to put the questioner of meaning on the alert. For though the emphasis changes with the passing of time, words, like people, can never lose altogether any part of their past. "Obsolete" meanings are not quite obsolete; they have just gone underground, and continue to exert an obscure influence. It is interesting, and not at all irrelevant to the study of the total meaning of "sadness," that among its ancient definitions are such concepts as "seriousness" and "importance" and "firmness." In Shropshire today, the expression "in good sadness" means "firmly, seriously, indeed and in fact." And in fourteenth-century England, to sleep or to drink sadly did not mean to do so dolefully, but with commendable thoroughness.

In twentieth-century American, however, "sadness" is not at all commendable. One has only to be in a reflective mood, or in some way occupied with serious thought, to elicit from friend or stranger the protest, "Why are you so sad?"—as if one were committing some kind of social sin. Is it really wrong to be serious? Could there be any pity, sympathy, mercy, or compassion in the world without a certain sadness, a taste of the suffering of others? It can even be said that no true joy is possible without it, either.

The more we examine words as the symbols of ideas, the clearer it becomes that there are no synonyms. The study of their derivations and usages shows a range of related meanings widening to some whole we can never reach with words, but which words—if we respect them enough in their differences and their relationships, and try to deal honestly with both—can powerfully help us to approach.

But if aspects of the same thing cannot contradict each other, how can we understand that sadness can mean both having too much and not having enough? This question seems to lead us to the heart of our experience, and reveals that aspect of sadness which we have found the least obvious and the most interesting. It has to do, perhaps, with a "cosmic suffering," and the only escape from it, for it refers to the different levels of our outer and inner worlds. We have, indeed, too much of what is not enough; and the sadness of our "not enough" is not on the same plane as the sadness of our "too much." Maybe the lack we are most aware of (and what we seem to suffer from the most) is of this world's goods or good fortune; but our suffering from such deprivation, whether imaginary or terribly real, is something other than true sadness. It is when we begin to feel that the problems and values of this world take up too much room, carry too much weight in relation to other more inner wishes; when we become aware of both our worlds at once, and know that we are overfilled, overwhelmed, overcome on this level of daily life, and in the inner life there is a great lack, a great hunger; when we experience this, our inevitable human situation, this, I think, is sadness.

Thomas Buckley has written that anger (with God, with life, and with oneself) must change to sadness: this state of seeing and acknowledging what is seen; accepting, but not with the sense of "resignation." What, then, must sadness turn into, in the process of a developing understanding? This state of seeing truly how things are, with us and with the world, is like a landing on a stairway, from which we can go either up or down. We can go very easily from sadness to depression, despondency, self-pity, despair, and all the blackest, most useless, most destructive forms of negativity. Or the vision of how things are can come as the bearer of light, and be essentially useful for continuing a search for understanding. Out of this sadness of seeing—and perhaps not from any other source—can come a need, and a reaching up for that possible relationship between our two worlds that, in giving sense to the one and reality to the other, could reveal to us a new world and our place in it as truly human beings.

TRANSITION:
POEMS 1926-1977

The Crystal Skull

I am bone:
bright bone, translucent bone, aware
of soft opacity of flesh, but separate:
older than flesh and longer lasting
I bone have a different destiny.

Alone, aware
bone does not care
for skin's sensation
knows but is free
of colored pictures dancing in the mind.

Bone thinks and feels
by what the marrow knows:
informed and fed by secret nerve and blood,
lit, fired from within to find
exact articulation
structure's precise and beautiful affirmative:

bone to its bone stand up:
these bones shall live.

Levavi Oculos Meos...

I shall lift up my head and go
Among the hills and live in loneliness
And listen for the silent voice of God
In the loud water falling on the rocks
And see his hands stretched out among the
  boughs
And I shall say no word, but worship there.

One day I shall come quietly back to you
With speech a sweet new thing upon my tongue
And words like new-winged birds, lovely and
  strange and slow.

The Journey

Sharp is the spur my master wears
And sharp the pain I feel
When my reluctant side he tears
With his unpitying heel;
Yet, Lord, spare not the steel,
For if I lack the goad
I will not take the road.

Drive me with pain the dusty miles,
Compel me to the race,
Nor let me stop to graze awhile
Nor ever change my pace
Until I reach the place
Whence the road led before—
The stable's open door;

The welcoming manger heaped with hay
Where such as I once stood,
Stabled and tired at end of day,
Munched straw, and chewed the cud,
And saw, in dust and blood,
In pain and humbleness,
That Stranger born to us.

Frijoles Canyon: Nov. 5, 1949

Death walks in the canyon under the stealthy
   moon; his track
patterned with buzzards' claws. A sudden
   thunder
shattering the dark,
the terrified hoofs of deer running from the
   silent pursuer:
the shadow crouches under the rock, claws bared
   to rend.
On the dim cliff a spark;
a ghost-fire gleams
in some old cave whose dwellers long ago
went out to a bloody end.
Yesterday's sun has sunk forever under,
tomorrow's will not rise:
only the moonlight cold on the mountain's
   shoulder.

Up in the sacred cavern the shadows hang
   like bats
black in the moon the shrine's mouth gapes
   horror
breath rattles in the throat.
Run, run with the deer in the dark, the light
   is gone,
death comes on black wings, on pads, on
   fleshless feet:
there is nothing but death in the dark, and the
   cheating moon:

tomorrow's sun will never rise
the sun is gone . . .
silence and the thudding heart . . .

Wait.
Open your eyes:
it is all quiet, only the heart sounds,
the footsteps and the wingbeats are no more:
fear has withdrawn.
Framed in the cave's long arch the patient
    mountains shine:
behold the mute obedience of the trees.
Now from the shrine
breathes out the incense of an ancient prayer.
Listen: that voice rides on the quiet air.

Go now in peace. The ghosts are your brothers:
did you not know before?
You may warm your hands at their fires.
The deer stand at the pool, gazing with liquid
    eyes:
touch them if you will, the antlered head
bows to your hand.
Out of the ledge the mountain lion slides
to stretch beside you, rubbing in the sand.
Between the canyon walls across the sky
golden Orion strides.

Paracas

Sea pulses with the sun,
sand and wind drift
earth water fire and air
blend, shift;
the moving sands pour color echoing tone:

Echo of woven cloth and hollowed bone
the desert sings
into the sky, into the changing sea
bluegreen against the cliffs dark gold and wine
sandmoulded stone:

Colors of air and fire and water pouring
down the dunes drift like liquid sound
stone hollowing: caves resound
to sea drums, ocean chords, sea-lions roaring:

Echo of men long gone from cloth and bone
and all the patterns of their death and birth
return as color moving, song
of woven fire and water, air and earth.

The Sleeping Prince

The prince dreams in the garden by the fountain,
His eyes no longer remember the sky, nor his
  hand the sword,
he has forgotten his castle and its people,
they have forgotten their lord.

The servants quarrel,
the men-at-arms laze in the sun by the wall,
the body-guards sprawled at the high table
feed on the king's fare in the king's own hall,
eat drink and laugh, or ride out to plunder:

the prince stirs in his dream, light as a narrow leaf
  on grass,
and the guards start pale hearing a sound like far-
  off thunder,
feeling the ground shake; then stillness again, and
  the terrors pass,
and they return to drink and games and laughter
passing the cup by turns and playing at king
and the prince dreams on in the neglected garden
where birds and fountains sing.

What will rouse you, prince, what bell or bugle
or till your death-hour will you not stir from sleep?
when the enemy swarms the walls, and the light
  from your burning castle
shines on the blades at your throat, and only the
  fountains weep.

Christmas Gift

Now in the cave the child is born:
even the beasts rejoice
and there are kings and laboring men
who know enough to kneel to him.

You and I, what bring we then?
We without eyes or voice,
without a song to sing?

We bring the nails, the thorn
to crown him king.

Dream of a Mountain

The ridge climbed toward a peak we never
  reached.
On both sides roared the wind.
Where the peak soared, air thinned,
no wind shifted the glittering cloud,
lifted the snow's hem with delicate fingerings,
but where we were
it drove down the enormous slopes of air
shouting so loud
feet staggered, but the heart rode on wings.
We never reached that windless crest . . .
  breath weak,
laboring heart, feet numb;
but oh! the crying wind below that peak
where no cries come.

The House

The house stands empty in the hollow dark:
blank stare the windows and the door is barred.
Weeds grow in the yard.
But I saw a crack of light under the door,
I heard footsteps that jarred.

They said, "You are crazy; there is no one there;
you heard the wind perhaps, or bats, or a mouse;
the house has been vacant for years—
   you can see the stair
tented with cobwebs, bare...
A light? In an empty house?"
               Yet, under the bolted door
I saw the light; I felt the floor
shake with the footfall.
There is someone there.

To My Son

My pulse beat in your echoing vein
while dumb and bound you lay in me,
your body's nerves spoke to my brain;
now for a short space you are free
from the soft prison of the womb.
You must go forth, take dangerous breath,
inhabiting a wider room
in the world's house; this is my door
you enter through; the walls are strange.
On either side, the winds of change
beat down the boughs you look upon,
and I may shelter you no more;
having now made you, blood and bone,
a harp to sing between those winds,
no more are the plucked strings my own.
It is your music they will sound;
I wait and listen for the song.

The Immortals

I went through the forest and saw two horses
  standing
Tethered with a silver rope to a cedar tree:
The fair horse of day, with white mane gleaming,
The stallion of the night, as black as ebony.

They stood quietly, and made no sound nor
  motion,
But lifted up their timeless heads dark-eyed
  and sorrowful;
I would have put my hand on them, I would have
  touched them gently,
Save that they were so lovely, and that they
  stood so still.

And the Lord Taketh Away

Bury the hope.
Wind the white shroud
head and foot;
take for the price full paid, take in exchange
for the sweet wanted fruit
this bitter wine poured out.

Bury the hope.
Drop the black clod,
lift the cup...
Look up now from this grave, look up;
Blessed be Thy name, O God.

Sagebrush

Gray sage where autumn aspens burn
Green sage and white in sun and wind,
Sage silver under moon and star,
Sage growing where my footprints are
Now frosts have come and leaves have thinned
Keep well my steps till I return.

Down many canyons traveling
Quick water trembles over stones,
Fast fade the still-renewing snows
Inconstant as a briar-rose;
Still stand the hills, unshaken thrones,
The pines are green from spring to spring.

Over the unforgetting ground
The sagebrush blows in sun and rain
That feet of many men have pressed;
Remember mine among the rest
And hide until I come again
From other feet the paths I found.

Equinox

Plunging comes the dark horse rain,
he shakes the lightning from his mane,
he whisks aloft his windy tail;
sparks of lightning mark his trail
that his iron heels have riven
from the cobblestones of heaven.

Mortal horses on the plain
stamp and shiver in the rain,
lift the nostril, prick the ear,
pray the snorting god to hear:
Drop Thy bolts, O Deity,
break the fence and set us free.

The Deer

Silently poised, he stood
Like some old tapestry of far-off weaving
Between the painted trees in the dim wood,
The crowned head lifted, staring quietly.

I think that it was Pan who challenged me
With great eyes proudly still;
Nothing but God could be so beautiful.

August

The tree hung like an empty glove.
The sea lay like an unstruck gong.
The hollow sky curved down in brass
Darkening to the slow bronze thunder,
And dust lay waiting in the grass
For rain that did not come.

I wonder

If there is any heart worth love
Or any beauty worth a song.

Transition

Down what strange hill
to this lost track
twisting, white under the alien stars
how came I here?

Passing each tree, each stone
a shadow reaches back
something once known
I cannot now recall, it is too far
and the path starts
nowhere and drops off sheer

oh still
the question hangs again on the dead air
an echo spoken by no human tongue

down what strange hill
far from my home
where have I come?

Credits

The essays in this book were written as opening editorials, or "Focuses," for the following issues of PARABOLA Magazine:

"The Hero"	Vol. I, No. 1 1976
"Cosmology"	Vol. II, No. 3 1977
"Sacred Space"	Vol. III, No. 1 1978
"Magic"	Vol. I, No. 2 1976
"Death"	Vol. II, No. 1 1977
"Creation"	Vol. II, No. 2 1977
"Initiation"	Vol. I, No. 3 1976
"Rites of Passage"	Vol. I, No. 4 1976
"Sacrifice and Transformation"	Vol. III, No. 2 1978
"Obstacles"	Vol. V, No. 3 1980
"Ceremonies"	Vol. VII, No. 3 1982
"Pilgrimage"	Vol. IX, No. 3 1984
"Relationships"	Vol. II, No. 4 1977
"Androgyny"	Vol. III, No. 4 1978
"The Child"	Vol. IV, No. 3 1979
"Storytelling and Education"	Vol. IV, No. 4 1979
"Music, Sound, Silence"	Vol. V, No. 2 1980
"Mask and Metaphor"	Vol. VI, No. 3 1981
"Dreams and Seeing"	Vol. VII, No. 2 1982
"Wholeness"	Vol. X, No. 1 1985
"Attention"	Vol. XV, No. 2 1990
"Triad"	Vol. XIV, No. 4 1989
"Repetition and Renewal"	Vol. XIII, No. 2 1988
"Hospitality"	Vol. XV, No. 4 1990
"Time and Presence"	Vol. XV, No. 1, 1990
"Sadness"	Vol. XI, No. 3 1986

Poems

PARABOLA, the Magazine of Myth and Tradition, is published quarterly by the Society for the Study of Myth and Tradition. For subscription information or to order back issues, address correspondence to PARABOLA, 656 Broadway, New York, NY 10012-2317.